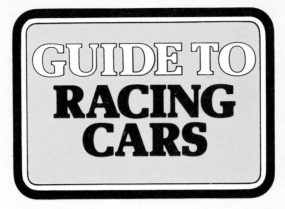

GUIDE TO
RACING CARS

Nigel Roebuck

Illustrated by Tom Brittain,
James Dugdale and Cliff Meadway

Designed by Vanessa Clarke

Ray Rourke Publishing Company, Inc.
Windermere, Florida 32786

Published by Ray Rourke Publishing Company, Inc.,
Windermere, Florida 32786.
Library of Congress Cataloging in Publication Data

Roebuck, Nigel.
  Guide to racing cars.

  (Explorer guides)
  Includes index.
  SUMMARY: An introduction to race cars and some
types of racing.
    1. Automobiles, Racing—Juvenile literature.
2. Automobile racing—Juvenile literature.   [1. Auto-
mobiles, Racing.   2. Automobile racing.]   I. Brittain,
Tom.   II. Dugdale, James, 1939-   .   III. Meadway,
Clifford.   IV . Title.
  TL236.R618   1981   629.2'28   81-539
  ISBN 0-86592-019-2   AACR1

Contents

About This Book

During the last few years, the popularity of motor racing has grown at a tremendous rate. An average Grand Prix crowd today is around 100,000. And the names of the stars are well known in many countries. All the big teams, like Lotus and Ferrari, attract their own devoted fans.

Motor racing is not only for Grand Prix cars, however. Before reaching Formula 1, the top class of the sport, a driver must first gain experience in other less powerful cars. This book sets out to introduce the young fan to all levels of the sport.

What to Look For

When you see *Formula* 1 Grand Prix cars for the first time, they will probably all look much the same to you, different only in color. But there are distinct differences, and after a time you will spot them more easily.

Many aspects are common to all Grand Prix cars, however. Now that the curious six-wheeled Tyrrell has disappeared, all have four wheels. All are rear-engined, and all have a large rear *wing* and front *spoiler* to improve roadholding. All cars must have a *rollbar* at the back of the cockpit and safety belts to protect the driver in an accident. The cars are all driven by the rear wheels, which are much bigger than those at the front.

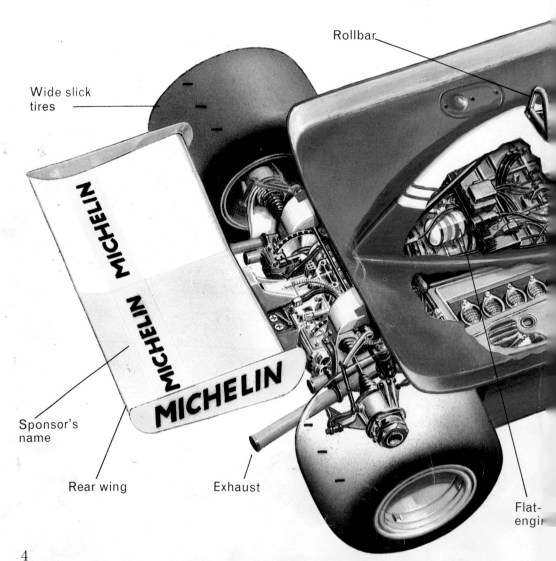

Rollbar

Wide slick tires

Sponsor's name

Rear wing

Exhaust

Flat-engine

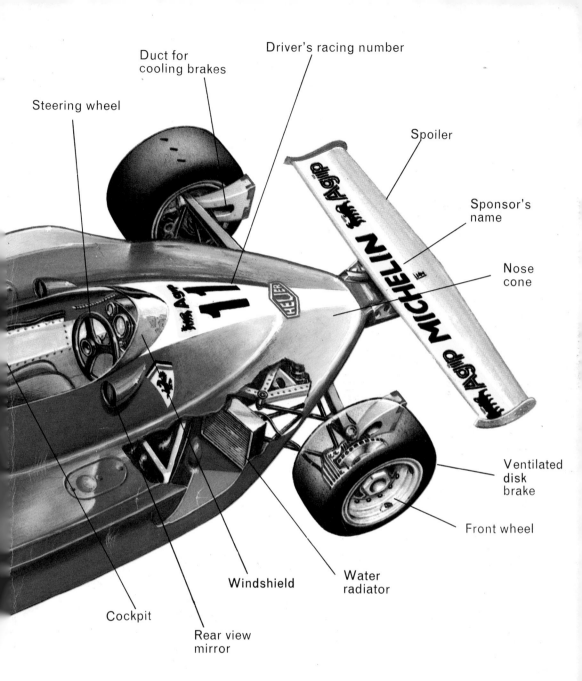

Duct for
cooling brakes

Driver's racing number

Steering wheel

Spoiler

Sponsor's
name

Nose
cone

Ventilated
disk
brake

Front wheel

Water
radiator

Windshield

Cockpit

Rear view
mirror

▲ **Ferrari 312T3** This car, powered by a 3-liter,
12-cylinder engine, produces about 520-horse-
power. In 1978, the car scored five Grand Prix
wins. It was driven by Argentina's Carlos
Reutemann and Canada's Gilles Villeneuve.

Classic Racing Cars

▲ **7·6-liter Peugeot, 1912** (France) Driven by Boillot, the 1912 French Grand Prix winner.

In the course of motor racing's 70-year history, just a few cars have earned the right to be called "classics", as a result of their successes. Some, such as the 1962 Lotus 25, scored highly because of technical innovations. The Lotus, for example, was the first car of the modern era to have a *monocoque* construction. This is now a standard feature of all Grand Prix cars. Other cars are included here simply because they dominated racing at a particular time.

▶ **4·5-liter Bentley, 1928** (England) The Bentley team dominated at Le Mans from 1927 to 1930, winning the 24-hour race each time. Woolf Barnato and Bernard Rubin were the drivers in 1928.

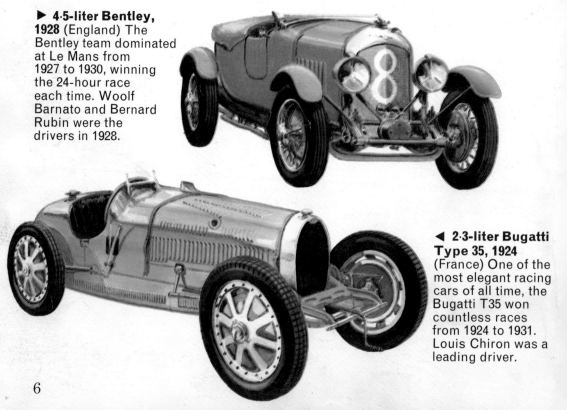

◀ **2·3-liter Bugatti Type 35, 1924** (France) One of the most elegant racing cars of all time, the Bugatti T35 won countless races from 1924 to 1931. Louis Chiron was a leading driver.

▼ **5·6-liter Mercedes-Benz W125, 1937** (Germany) The most powerful Grand Prix car of its time.

▲ **6·0-liter Auto-Union C-type, 1936** (Germany) Driven by Bernd Rosemeyer, it won most 1936 Grand Prix.

▼ **Alfa Romeo 158/9, 1950** (Italy) The great Juan Fangio won the 1950 World Championship in a 159.

▼ **2-liter Ferrari 500F2, 1952/3** (Italy) It took world titles in 1952/3, driven by Alberto Ascari.

▲ **2·5-liter Maserati 250F, 1957** (Italy) Used by Fangio to win the 1957 World Championship.

▼ **1·5-liter Lotus 25, 1962** (England) The fastest car of 1962, driven by Scotsman Jimmy Clark.

◀ **McLaren M26** Driven by Britain's James Hunt in 1978.

▲ **Brabham BT46** Niki Lauda's car for the 1978 Grand Prix.

Formula 1 Cars

Formula 1 cars, which compete every year for the World Championship, are regarded as the best racing cars. They are powered by 3-liter engines of either eight or twelve cylinders. The typical Formula 1 Grand Prix car is very light, but it carries an enormous amount of power.

A typical Grand Prix race has 24 starters. About half of these will finish the race two hours later. The rest will have dropped out because of either accidents or mechanical failures. Often, Grand Prix are won on reliability rather than speed because of the great strain on the mechanical parts of the cars.

▶ **Tyrrell 008** In Patrick Depailler's hands, this car won the 1978 Monaco Grand Prix.

▼ **Ligier-Matra JS9** All-French Formula 1 car, piloted by Jacques Laffite in 1978.

▶ Lotus 79
Mario Andretti drove it to six Grand Prix wins – and the World Championship – in 1978.

◀ Ferrari 312T3
Driven by Carlos Reutemann and Gilles Villeneuve, it won five 1978 Grand Prix.

Most of the present-day Formula 1 Grand Prix cars are powered by the Ford-Cosworth DFV engine. This engine now has more than 100 Grand Prix wins to its credit. But there are a few exceptions to the rule. Ferrari use their own flat-12 engine and the Brabham team use Alfa Romeo engines in their cars.

Ligier, from France, have used the Matra 12-cylinder engine, while the Renault team have their own *turbocharged* six-cylinder unit. All the teams use Goodyear or Michelin tires, which have different surfaces for different conditions. The cars run on ordinary fuel.

USAC Indianapolis Formula

The cars in this formula are powered by Cosworth or Offenhauser engines and can reach speeds of over 200 mph. Most events take place on oval tracks in the United States and Canada. The most famous race is the Indianapolis 500 (805 km).

▼ Penske PC6 Driven by Tom Sneva to win the 1978 USAC Championship.

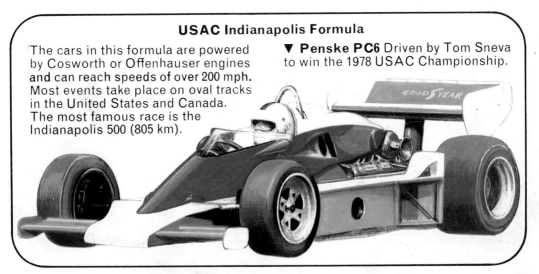

Other Single Seaters

Single-seater Formula 1 cars are the best-known class of racing cars. But there are several other single-seater types. These lower formulas, such as Formula Ford, Formula 3 and Formula 2 also attract the crowds. And it is in these classes that tomorrow's Grand Prix drivers make their names.

Motor racing at all levels is extremely expensive, and this is the main reason for the success of Formula Ford. It enables a young driver to gain experience in a single-seater racing car, at quite low cost. The engines used are really the same as those in the ordinary Ford car.

If successful in Formula Ford, the driver then hopes to move to Formula 3. These cars are very like Formula 1 cars. But they are smaller and much less powerful. Formula 2, with 300-horsepower cars, is the final stepping-stone to every driver's ambition – Formula 1 and the Grand Prix World Championship. Few drivers get that far.

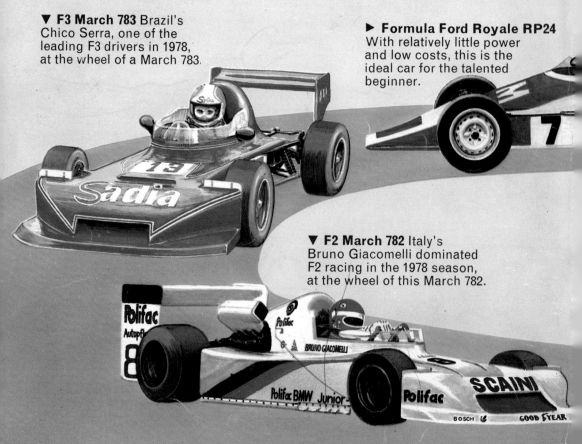

▼ **F3 March 783** Brazil's Chico Serra, one of the leading F3 drivers in 1978, at the wheel of a March 783.

▶ **Formula Ford Royale RP24** With relatively little power and low costs, this is the ideal car for the talented beginner.

▼ **F2 March 782** Italy's Bruno Giacomelli dominated F2 racing in the 1978 season, at the wheel of this March 782.

Drag Racing

Drag racing started many years ago in the United States. It is now popular in Europe. Dragsters are designed purely for straight-line speed, the quickest reaching over 200 mph in less than six seconds!

▲ **Slingshot dragster** A typical top-class dragster – with more than 1000-horsepower.

▶ **F2 Chevron B42** One of the quickest F2 cars, the Chevron has had much recent success.

▼ **F3 Ralt RT1** British driver Derek Warwick scored many F3 victories in 1978, driving a Ralt RT1 throughout the year.

11

Sports Cars

Sadly, sports car racing is not as popular as it used to be. Many car companies which once took part have withdrawn, for example, Jaguar, Ferrari, Maserati and Aston Martin.

Nevertheless, sports car races are still held. By far the most important is the legendary Le Mans 24 Hours, run in June each year. In the last few years the leading competitors have been Porsche and Renault. Both teams use cars with very powerful, turbo-charged engines, giving top speeds of more than 200 mph. All sports cars are divided into classes according to size and power. In some events production cars (modified road cars) also compete.

▲ **Ford Mk IV, 1967** Used by Dan Gurney and A J Foyt to win at Le Mans in 1967.

▲ **Porsche 935, 1978** Driven by Jacky Ickx and Jochen Mass, the fastest 1978 sports car.

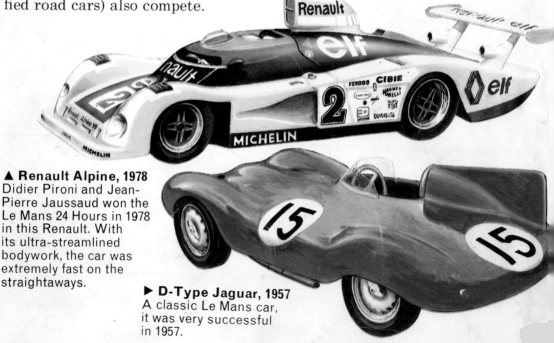

▲ **Renault Alpine, 1978** Didier Pironi and Jean-Pierre Jaussaud won the Le Mans 24 Hours in 1978 in this Renault. With its ultra-streamlined bodywork, the car was extremely fast on the straightaways.

▶ **D-Type Jaguar, 1957** A classic Le Mans car, it was very successful in 1957.

▲ **BMW CSL** Dominated the
European Touring Car Championship.

▲ **VW Scirocco** The fastest sedan
car in its class during 1978.

Can-Am Racing

As its name suggests, Can-Am
racing is confined to Canada
and the USA. The cars are single-
seaters, but have sports car-type
bodywork, and nearly all are
powered by Chevrolet engines.
Alan Jones's Lola T333CS (above)
was a clear championship winner
in 1978.

Stock Cars

Stock cars are highly modified sedans,
designed to race on banked oval tracks
at speeds of 200 mph. Richard Petty,
Cale Yarborough and David Pearson
are among the leading drivers. Chevrolet,
Ford, Dodge and Mercury are the fastest
cars. The races, up to 600 miles long,
are mostly in the southern states.

▼ **Mercury Cyclone** Driven
by David Pearson (USA).

Sedans

Sedan car racing has always been tremendously popular in Europe. For the races are usually very hard-fought affairs and the cars look very much like family sedans.

The cars are usually modified. This means that their engines are tuned for higher speeds. There are rules controlling modifications for championship events, but still some cars are capable of more than 140 mph. The races are divided into classes with the Ford Capris and BMWs in the top class, the Dolomites in the next, and Alfasuds and Minis in the small class.

▲ **Mini 1275GT** A regular and successful racing sedan for the last 15 years.

▼ **Alfasud Ti** Usually the fastest car in the small class.

▼ **European stock car races** are run on dirt tracks. The cars are old sedans, with special engines and strengthened chassis.

▼ Triumph Dolomite Sprint
The Dolomite has only a
2-liter engine, but it is among
the fastest cars in its class.

▲ VW Golf GTi A successful
German racing sedan.

► Ford Capri Nearly always
the fastest cars in the
race, the Capris have had
tremendous success.

Rallies, Rallycross and Hillclimbs

Rallying is another popular form of motor sport. Many of the world's largest car companies enter teams in the big events such as the Monte Carlo and RAC Rallies.

Motor companies such as Ford, Fiat, Saab and Toyota are fierce rivals in European Rally Championship events. The results are decided on the times recorded on "special stages". These sometimes take place on asphalt roads and sometimes on dirt roads through forestry land. The weather also plays a vital part. The drivers sometimes have to contend with snow and ice, and at other times with blazing heat.

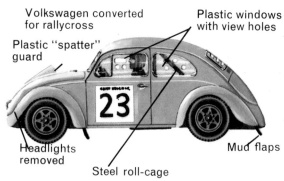

Volkswagen converted for rallycross

Plastic windows with view holes

Plastic "spatter" guard

Headlights removed

Steel roll-cage

Mud flaps

▲ **Rallycross** is a popular sport in Europe today. Compared to rallies, events are short in length. Rounds of the European Championship are run in Germany, Belgium, Holland, France and Britain. The outside of the cars looks very similar to normal rally cars, but there are differences. The rally-cross cars are very light as all surplus weight has been stripped off. The engines have been altered, and the cars must have a steel roll-cage inside for the driver's safety. Tires must suit both paved and dirt surfaces.

Notebook

Stopwatch

Pencil

Going to a Rally

When watching a rally – particularly a "special stage" through forestry land – the first rule is to stand somewhere safe. Never, for instance, stand on the outside of a corner, and never cross the track. Take a stopwatch with you, to time the drivers through your section, and keep a notebook handy to write down the times.

Hillclimbing is a very specialized branch of motor sport. The cars do not compete with each other, but only against the clock. Timing is very important, as the results are often only a hundredth of a second apart!

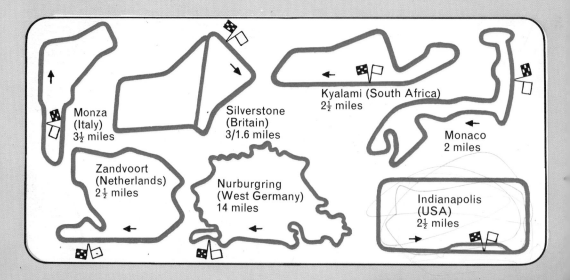

Monza
(Italy)
3½ miles

Silverstone
(Britain)
3/1.6 miles

Kyalami (South Africa)
2¼ miles

Monaco
2 miles

Zandvoort
(Netherlands)
2½ miles

Nurburgring
(West Germany)
14 miles

Indianapolis
(USA)
2½ miles

The Circuits

Motor racing meetings are held on circuits all over the world. Some of these circuits are illustrated above, but not all of them are in use today.

At any circuit, the best place to watch a race is from one of the grandstands where you can look down on the track. But if you arrive early you can probably get a good place by the spectator fence. Try and find somewhere near the pit area. You can then see the mechanics at work and also watch the start and finish of a race. Notice the medical and firefighting units at the corners of the circuit. Flag *marshals* also stand there to keep a watch on the condition of the track. Remember, motor racing is dangerous, so never climb over the safety fence.

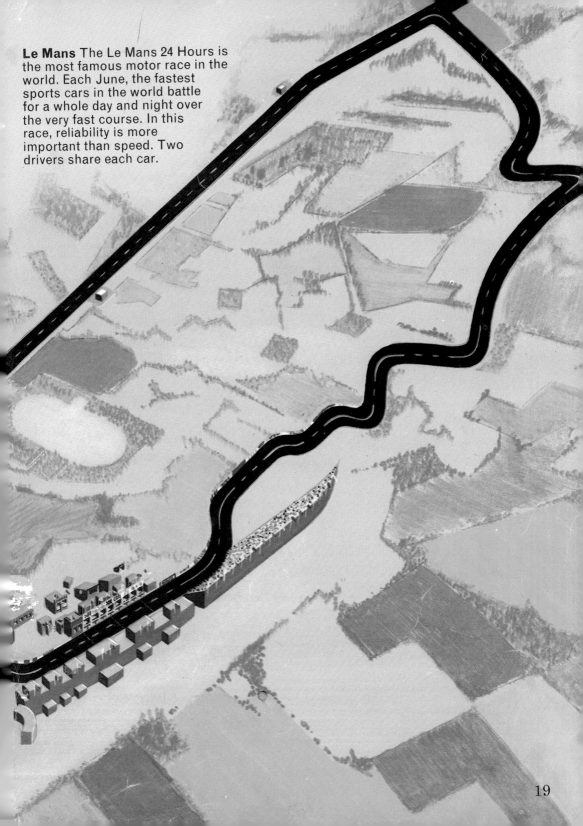

Le Mans The Le Mans 24 Hours is the most famous motor race in the world. Each June, the fastest sports cars in the world battle for a whole day and night over the very fast course. In this race, reliability is more important than speed. Two drivers share each car.

▲ **Blue flag** This means that a following driver is trying to pass.

▲ **Yellow and red flag** Oil on the circuit. Slow down through this section.

▲ **Black flag** This means that the driver must stop at his pit on the next lap.

At the Races

The best way of keeping track of a race is to make a lap chart. This is a list of all the drivers and the numbers of their cars. Make a note of the car numbers as they pass you. Take a stopwatch with you and see if you can time the gaps between the cars.

Try and get a pit area pass. You can then walk through the area where the cars are being prepared for the race. The drivers will also be there, so take your autograph book with you.

Pit Signals

Pit signals are held out to drivers during the race. They tell them various things, such as the lap number and the time gap to the next car.

▲ **Yellow flag** Danger. Slow down through this section.

▲ **Red flag** Race stopped. Pull up at once.

▲ **Checkered flag** Waved at the winner. The race is over.

Pit stops are interesting to watch. The mechanics can change all four wheels in a matter of seconds. Each team keeps spare wheels, cans of fuel, spare wings, and, of course, different kinds of tools. Races have been won and lost on pit stops.

21

The Drivers' Helmets

▲ **Mario Andretti** (USA) World Champion in 1978. Won in Argentina, France, Spain, Belgium, Holland, Germany. Drives for Lotus.

▲ **Patrick Depailler** (France) Won the Monaco Grand Prix in 1978, driving for Tyrrell. Now drives a Ligier.

▲ **Emerson Fittipaldi** (Brazil) World Champion in 1972 and 1974. Now drives for his own team, Copersucar-Fittipaldi.

▲ **James Hunt** (Great Britain) World Champion in 1976, driving a McLaren. He now drives for the Wolf team.

▲ **Niki Lauda** (Austria) World Champion in 1975, 1977, in a Ferrari. Won in Sweden and Italy in 1978. Now drives for Brabham.

▲ **Gilles Villeneuve** (Canada) A rising young star, who won the Canadian Grand Prix. He drives for Ferrari.

▲ **Carlos Reutemann** (Argentina) Won in Brazil, Britain and America in 1978, in a Ferrari. Now drives for Lotus.

▲ **Jody Scheckter** (South Africa) One of the world's fastest drivers. Seven Grand Prix victories. Now drives for Ferrari.

▲ **John Watson** (Great Britain) Very successful in 1978, in a Brabham. Now drives for the team McLaren.

Glossary

Back marker A slow car running near the back of the race.

Chicane A man-made S-bend to reduce speeds before a very fast corner.

Drift Controlled four-wheel slide through a corner.

Formula A set of rules for a class of racing car.

Grid The order, determined by practice lap times, in which the cars start the race.

Guardrail A metal barrier built along edge of track to prevent cars sliding into spectator areas.

Line The fastest route through a corner.

Marshals Officials stationed around the course who give flag signals to the drivers, and assist in rescue work after accidents.

Monocoque means "single-shell". It is a term used for a system of building cars that does away with a separate chassis or frame. Instead the whole car's body is used to provide strength.

Pace lap A slow lap by all competing cars, in formation, immediately before the start of the race.

Qualifying Lapping sessions before the race when each car's lap time is recorded to determine the starting order for the race.

Rollbar A bend of tubular steel behind the cockpit to protect the driver if the car overturns.

Slipstreaming means following another car very closely at high speed to take advantage of decreased wind resistance.

Spoiler An airfoil mounted at the front of racing cars to increase down-force on the car. It improves roadholding and cornering speed.

T-car Car held in reserve by team in case primary car has a fault before the race.

Turbocharged A car with a turbine blower which pushes more air-fuel mixture into the engine to give more power.

Wing An airfoil mounted at the front and rear of racing cars to increase down-force on the car.

Index